JOHANNES BRAHMS

SCHICKSALSLIED
SONG OF DESTINY

(Friedrich Hölderlin)

für Chor und Orchester
op. 54

Klavierauszug / Vocal Score

EIGENTUM DES VERLEGERS · ALLE RECHTE VORBEHALTEN
ALL RIGHTS RESERVED

C. F. PETERS

FRANKFURT/M. · Leipzig · LONDON · NEW YORK

Schicksalslied
(Friedrich Hölderlin)

Ihr wandelt droben im Licht
Auf weichem Boden, selige Genien!
Glänzende Götterlüfte
Rühren Euch leicht,
Wie die Finger der Künstlerin
Heilige Saiten.

Schicksallos, wie der schlafende
Säugling, atmen die Himmlischen;
Keusch bewahrt
In bescheidener Knospe
Blühet ewig
Ihnen der Geist,
Und die seligen Augen
Blicken in stiller,
Ewiger Klarheit.

Doch uns ist gegeben,
Auf keiner Stätte zu ruh'n;
Es schwinden, es fallen
Die leidenden Menschen
Blindlings von einer
Stunde zur andern,
Wie Wasser von Klippe
Zu Klippe geworfen,
Jahrlang ins Ungewisse hinab.

Song of Destiny
(Friedrich Hölderlin)

You walk on high in the light
On airy ground, ye blissful seraphim!
Breezes celestial and radiant
Caress you as lightly
As the harpist's fingers brushing
The sacred lyre.

Doomless, like infants in slumber,
Breathe the divinities;
Chastely wrapt
In humble buds,
Their indwelling spirit
Eternally flowers,
And their blissful eyes
Gaze on in silent and
Eternal clarity.

And yet – for us
There is no resting place.
An anguished mankind
Reels and plummets
Blindly from one
Hour to the next,
Like water flung
From crag to crag,
Plunged for years in the unfathomable deep.

(Translation: Bradford Robinson)

BESETZUNG / ORCHESTRATION

2 Flauti – 2 Oboi – 2 Clarinetti – 2 Fagotti
2 Corni – 2 Trombe – 3 Tromboni – Timpani
Violino I/II – Viola – Violoncello – Contrabbasso
Coro

Aufführungsdauer / Duration: ca. 16 Min.

Partitur / Full Score: EP 8948
Aufführungsmaterial käuflich oder leihweise / Orchestral material for purchase or hire

SCHICKSALSLIED

FRIEDRICH HÖLDERLIN

Johannes Brahms, Op. 54

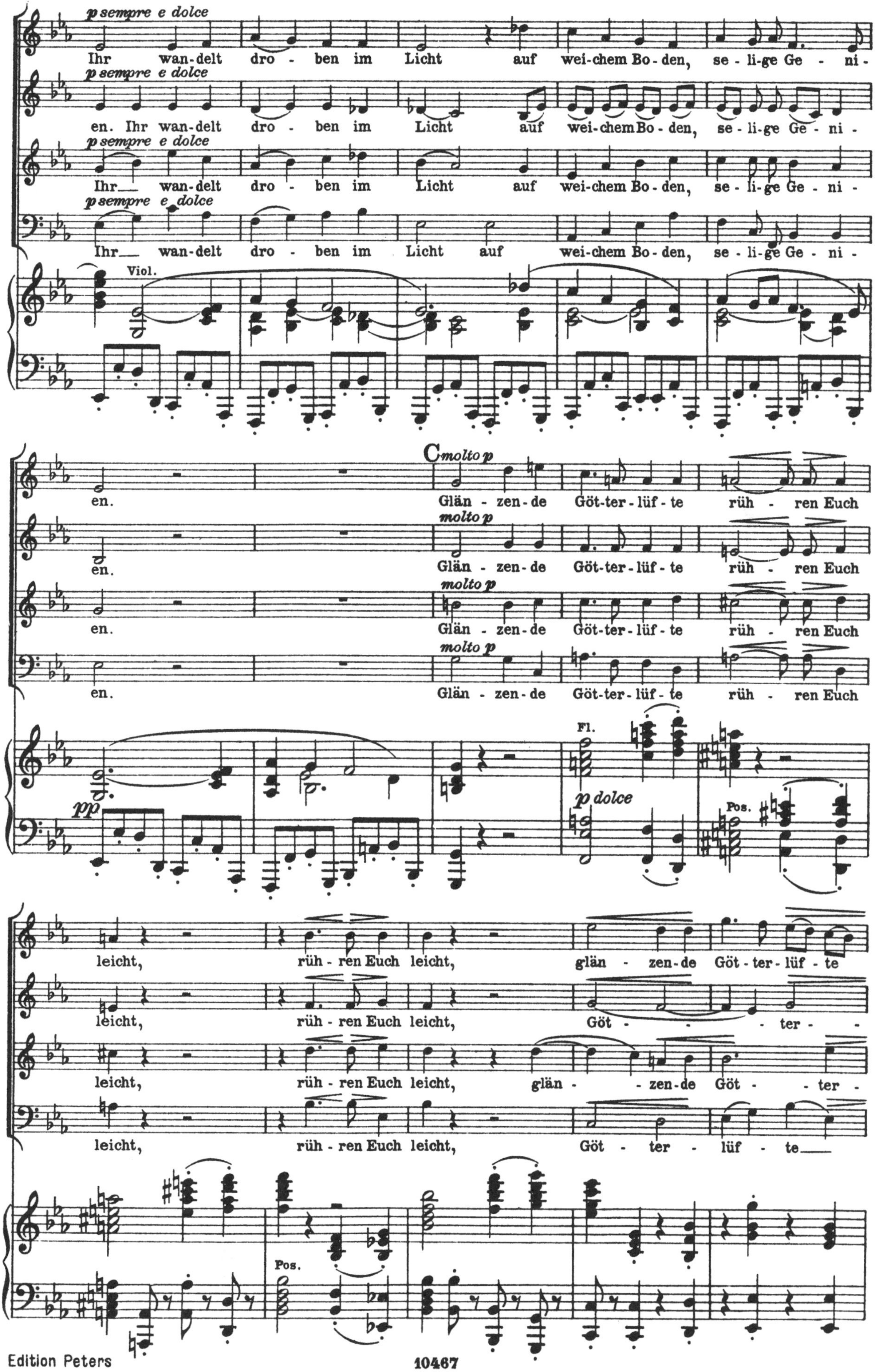

5

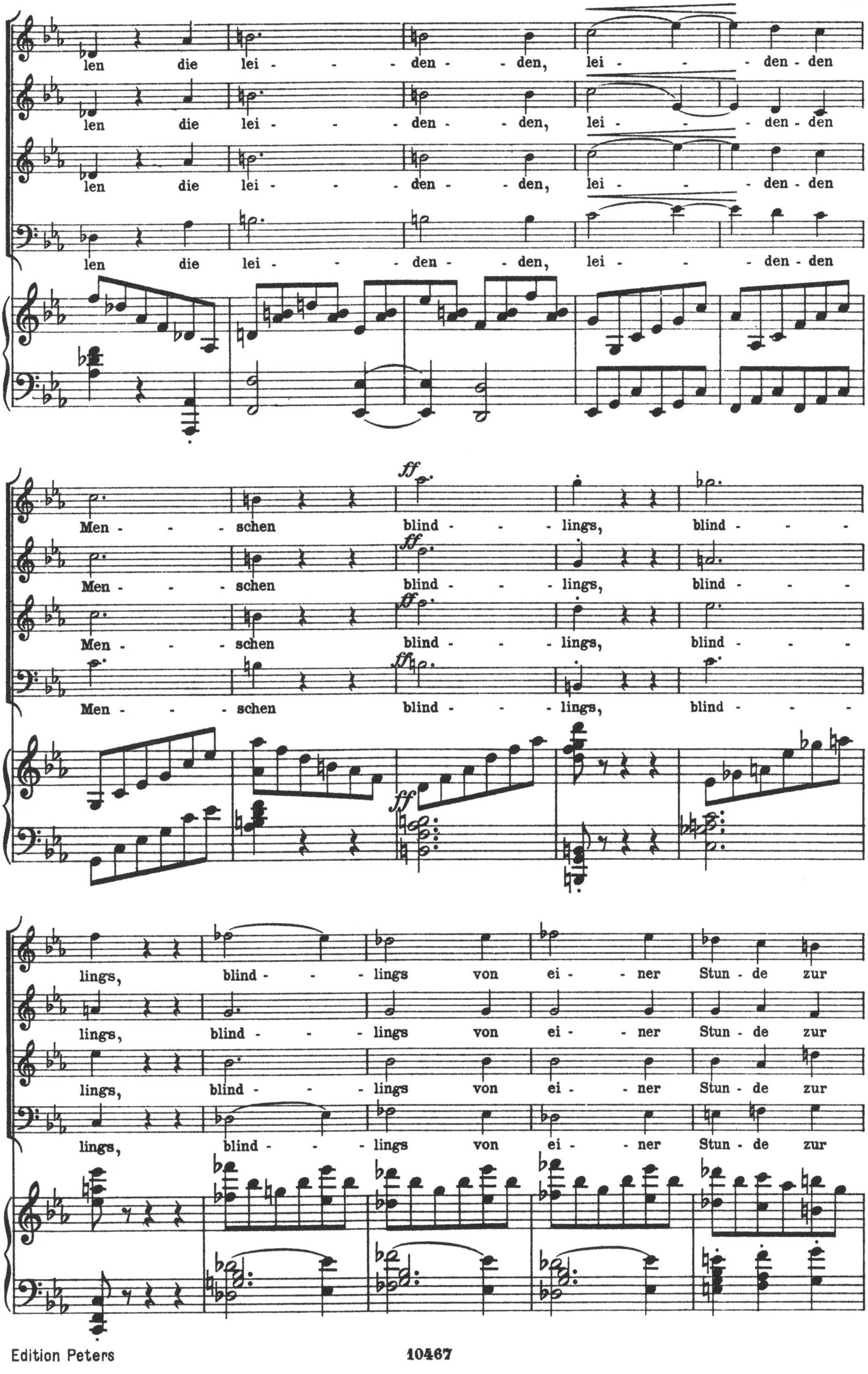
len die lei - - - den - - den, lei - - - den - den
len die lei - - - den - - den, lei - - - den - den
len die lei - - - den - - den, lei - - - den - den
len die lei - - - den - - den, lei - - - den - den
ff
Men - - - schen blind - - - lings, blind - - -
Men - - - schen blind - - - lings, blind - - -
Men - - - schen blind - - - lings, blind - - -
Men - - - schen blind - - - lings, blind - - -
ff
lings, blind - - - lings von ei - - ner Stun - de zur
lings, blind - - - lings von ei - - ner Stun - de zur
lings, blind - - - lings von ei - - ner Stun - de zur
lings, blind - - - lings von ei - - ner Stun - de zur

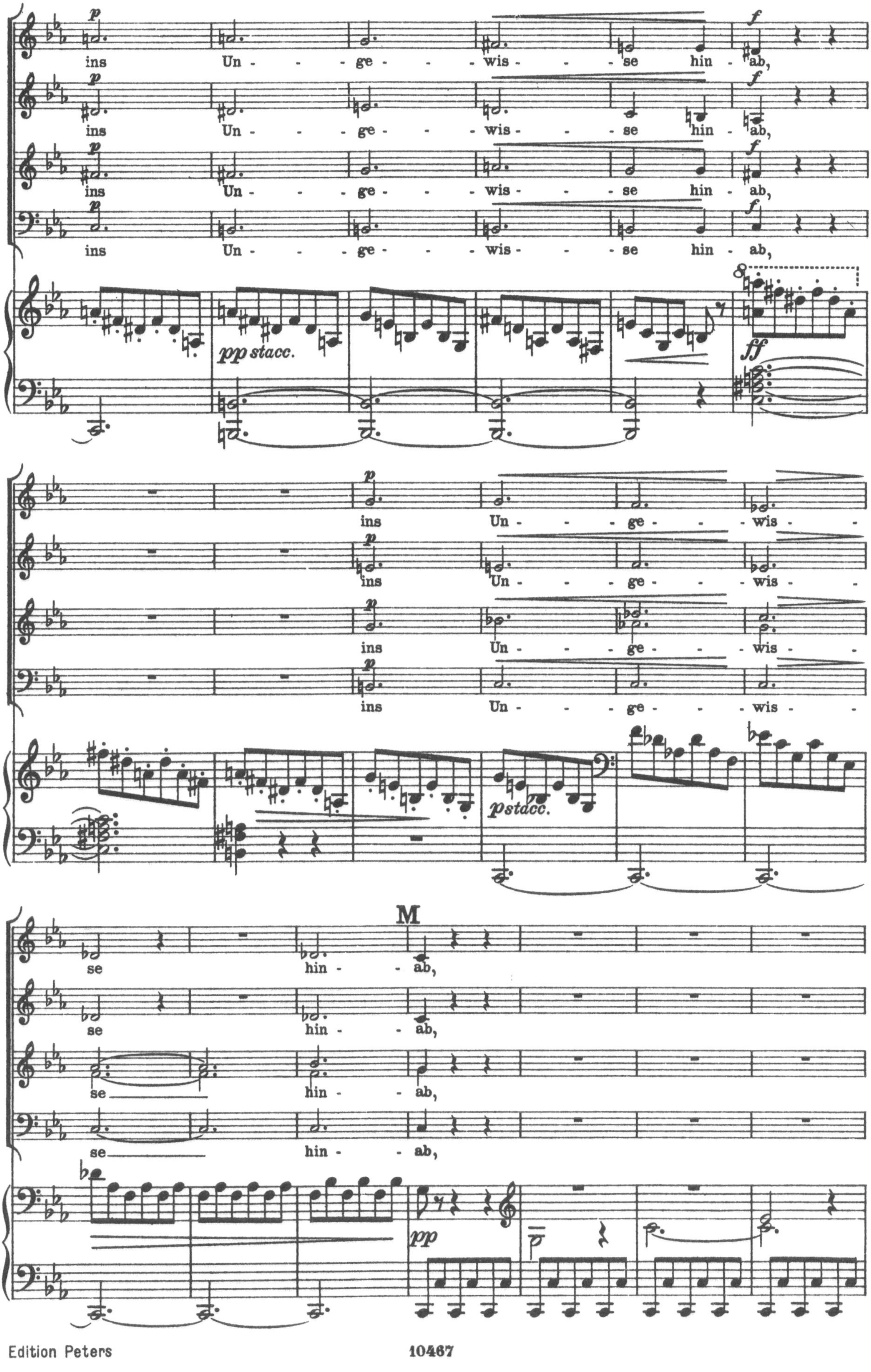
p
ins Un - - - ge - - - wis - - - se hin - ab,
f
ins Un - - - ge - - - wis - - - se hin - ab,
ins Un - - - ge - - - wis - - - se hin - ab,
pp stacc.
ff
ins Un - - - ge - - - wis -
ins Un - - - ge - - - wis -
p stacc.
M
se hin - - ab,
se hin - - ab,
pp

Nachwort

Das im Mai 1871 vollendete *Schicksalslied* op. 54 für Chor und Orchester von Johannes Brahms gehört zur Gattung der Weltlichen Kantate. Wegen der zentralen Rolle des Chores war diese Gattung von großer Bedeutung für die Musikkultur der zweiten Hälfte des 19. Jahrhunderts, die wesentlich durch die bürgerlichen Musik- und Chorvereinigungen geprägt wurde. Die hohen Aufführungszahlen belegen die schnelle Integration des Werkes in das Musikleben seiner Zeit. Nach der Uraufführung am 18. Oktober 1871 in Karlsruhe erklang das *Schicksalslied* bis zum Jahr 1880 weit über 30mal in den großen Konzertsälen Deutschlands, der Niederlande und der Schweiz.[1]

Wie allen seinen Weltlichen Kantaten hat Brahms auch dem *Schicksalslied* einen Text hohen literarischen Ranges zugrundegelegt. Mit dieser Textwahl entspricht er nicht nur der Erwartungshaltung des gebildeten Bürgertums, sondern er verweist auch auf den ästhetischen Anspruch, den er selbst mit seinen Chorwerken verbindet. Über die Textfindung und den Beginn der Komposition des Werkes berichtet Brahmsens Freund Albert Dietrich: *„Im Sommer [1868] kam Brahms noch einmal um mit Reinthaler's und uns einige Parthien in die Umgegend zu machen. Eines Morgens fuhren wir nach Wilhelmshaven, Brahms interessierte es, den großartigen Kriegshafen zu sehen. Unterwegs war der sonst so muntere Freund still und ernst. Er erzählte, er habe am Morgen (...) im Bücherschrank Hölderlin's Gedichte gefunden und sei von dem Schicksalslied auf das Tiefste ergriffen. Als wir später nach langem Umherwandern und nach Besichtigung aller interessanten Dinge ausruhend am Meere saßen, entdeckten wir bald Brahms in weiter Entfernung, einsam am Strand sitzend und schreibend. Es waren die ersten Skizzen des Schicksalsliedes (...). Eine schon geplante Parthie (...) unterblieb. Er eilte nach Hamburg zurück, um sich der Arbeit hinzugeben.“*[2]

Die Fertigstellung der Komposition wird Brahms bis ins Jahr 1871 beschäftigen, wobei ihm in der Hauptsache die Gestaltung des Schlusses große Probleme bereitete.

Das *Schicksalslied* ist deutlich in drei Teile gegliedert. Die ersten beiden Abschnitte entsprechen den Bildern der Dichtung Hölderlins. Zu Beginn beschwört Brahms die „ewige Klarheit" und Hoheit der Götterwelt, indem er den Chor nach einer in ruhiger Bewegung geführten, in stabilem Es-Dur gehaltenen Orchestereinleitung mit lichter Holzbläser- oder warmer Streicherinstrumentation verbindet. Im Gegensatz dazu steht der zweite, wahrhaft apokalyptische Teil für die von Leid erschütterte, dem Tode zustrebende Tragik des Menschenschicksals – „wie Wasser von Klippe zu Klippe geworfen, jahrlang ins Ungewisse hinab". Dissonante Harmonik, gegentaktige Rhythmik sowie eine sprunghafte, zerrissene Melodik bestimmen das furiose musikalische Geschehen.

Während Hölderlin in seinem Gedicht Götter- und Menschenwelt – ganz im Sinne des antiken Schicksalsbegriffes – unvereinbar nebeneinander bestehen läßt, kann Brahms diesen resignativen Schluß nicht akzeptieren. Er fügt dem zweiten Teil seines *Schicksalsliedes* eine Coda an, in der er den Einleitungsteil, nun nach C-Dur aufgehellt, aufgreift. Die Aussage des Hölderlinschen Textes wird dadurch wesentlich verändert – ins Versöhnliche gewendet.

Brahms hat lange an dem Schluß des Werkes gearbeitet und verschiedene Lösungen erwogen. Versuche, in denen der Chor Textzeilen des Anfangs wiederaufgreift oder gar die Idee, *„den Chor nur 'ah' singen zu lassen, quasi Brummstimen"*[3] wurden von ihm wieder verworfen. Ein Brief an den Freund Carl Reinthaler vom 24. Oktober 1871 verdeutlicht, daß Brahms auch bezüglich der schließlich gefundenen Fassung noch Zweifel hegte, denn er bezeichnet sie als möglicherweise mißlungenes Experiment: *„Das Schicksalslied wird gedruckt, und der Chor schweigt im letzten Adagio. Es ist eben – ein dummer Einfall oder was Du willst, aber es läßt sich nichts machen. Ich war so weit herunter, daß ich dem Chor was hineingeschrieben hatte; es geht ja nicht. Es mag so ein mißlungenes Experiment sein, aber durch solches Aufkleben würde ein Unsinn herauskommen. Wie wir genug besprochen: ich sage ja eben etwas, was der Dichter nicht sagt, und freilich wäre es besser, wenn ihm das Fehlende die Hauptsache gewesen wäre. –"*[4]

Die Neuerung, ein Chorwerk mit einem Orchesternachspiel enden zu lassen, rief Verwunderung unter den Zeitgenossen hervor. Die Kritik reagierte gespalten. Ablehnende Stimmen warfen Brahms vor, daß er die Intentionen Hölderlins durch den orchestralen Zusatz bis zur Unkenntlichkeit entstelle. Doch es gab auch positive Reaktionen, wie etwa die des bedeutenden Musikschriftstellers Hermann Kretzschmar, der den Schluß als den *„ethisch (...) vollständigen dritten Theil des Werkes"*[5] verstand. Wenn auch die Weltlichen Kantaten von Johannes Brahms, was ihren Bekanntheitsgrad betrifft, nicht an seine geistlichen Chorwerke – etwa das *Deutsche Requiem* – heranreichen, haben sie sich dennoch einen festen Platz im Konzertrepertoire bewahrt.

Marion Saxer

---

[1] Vgl. Angelika Horstmann, *Untersuchungen zur Brahms-Rezeption der Jahre 1860-1880*, Hamburg 1986, S. 195f.
[2] Zit. nach Siegfried Kross, *Johannes Brahms, Versuch einer kritischen Dokumentar-Biographie*, 2 Bde., Bonn 1997, S. 603.
[3] Max Kalbeck, *Johannes Brahms*, Bd. II, Berlin 1904-14, S. 366.
[4] Zit. nach Kross, *Johannes Brahms*, S. 604.
[5] Hermann Kretzschmar, *Neue Werke von J. Brahms* III, in: *Musikalisches Wochenblatt* 1874, Nr. 7, S. 83-97.

Postscript

Johannes Brahms's *Schicksalslied* op. 54 for chorus and orchestra, completed in May of 1871, belongs to the genre of the secular cantata. Due to the central role of the chorus, this genre was very important to the musical culture of the latter half of the nineteenth century, with its strong emphasis on bourgeois musical and choral societies. The large number of performances bears witness to the work's rapid integration in the musical life of its day. Following the première in Karlsruhe on 18 October 1871, it was given well over thirty times in the large concert halls of Germany, Switzerland and the Netherlands.[1]

As with all his secular cantatas, Brahms selected a text of high literary merit for his *Schicksalslied*. Not only did his choice accommodate the expectations of the educated classes, it is also indicative of the high artistic claims he raised for his choral music as a whole. An account of Brahms's discovery of the text and the work's early genesis is supplied by his friend Albert Dietrich: "In the summer [of 1868] Brahms arrived once again to undertake a couple of nearby outings with us and the Reinthalers. One morning we set out for Wilhelmshaven, where Brahms wanted to see the splendid naval harbor. During the journey our usually cheerful friend became quiet and serious. He explained that he had found Hölderlin's poetry (...) in the bookcase that morning and had been profoundly moved by the *Schicksalslied*. Later, after long walks and visits to all points of interest, we sat resting at the seaside and discovered Brahms a long distance away on the beach, sitting and writing. It was the initial sketches of his *Schicksalslied* (...). A planned outing (...) had to be cancelled. He rushed back to Hamburg to devote himself to his work."[2]

Brahms was probably occupied with the completion of the work until well into 1871. The shape of the conclusion in particular posed many problems.

The *Schicksalslied* falls clearly into three parts. The first two sections correspond to the imagery of Hölderlin's poem. At the opening the composer invokes the *ewige Klarheit* ("eternal clarity") and the majesty of the world of the gods by prefixing to the chorus a slow-moving orchestral introduction in a stable E-flat major, with delicate woodwind writing and warm string sonorities. In contrast, the truly apocalyptic second section stands for the tragic fate of humanity, stunned by suffering and hurtling toward death "like water flung from crag to crag, plunged for years in the unfathomable deep". Dissonant harmonies, jagged cross-rhythms and wide-leaping scraps of melody dominate the furious turmoil of the music.

While Hölderlin's poem juxtaposes the divine world unreconcilably with the human world – as was fully in keeping with the ancient concept of fate – Brahms was unable to accept this renunciatory conclusion. Instead, he appended to the second section of his *Schicksalslied* a coda that recapitulates the opening section, now transposed to C major. This considerably alters the meaning of Hölderlin's poem and adds the missing touch of reconciliation.

Brahms worked on this conclusion for a long time and considered various solutions. Some of his attempts, later rejected, have the chorus returning to lines from the opening, or even "singing 'ah' somewhat in the manner of a humming choir."[3] A letter of 24 October 1871 to his friend Carl Reinthaler reveals that Brahms still had doubts about his final version, which he referred to as a possibly failed experiment: "The Schicksalslied is about to be printed, and the chorus falls silent in the final adagio. Call it a stupid idea if you will, there is nothing to be done about it. I had fallen so low as to consider writing words in for chorus, but it wouldn't work. It may be a failed experiment, but tacking on new words would only have produced nonsense. As we already discussed at length: I am saying something that the poet does not say; and to be sure, it would be better if what he fails to say were the main point. –"[4]

The innovation of having a choral work end with an orchestral postlude occasioned puzzlement among Brahms's contem-poraries. The reviews were divided: negative critics accused Brahms of distorting Hölderlin's intentions beyond recognizability with his orchestral addendum. But there were also positive responses, such as those of the leading musicographer Hermann Kretzschmar, who viewed the conclusion as "the ethically (...) complete third section of the work."[5] If Brahms's secular cantatas cannot claim to reach the level of popularity of his sacred choral music – least of all the *German Requiem* – they have none the less earned a permanent place in the concert repertoire.

Marion Saxer

---

[1] See Angelika Horstmann, *Untersuchungen zur Brahms-Rezeption der Jahre 1860-1880* (Hamburg, 1986), p. 195f.
[2] Cite from Siegfried Kross, *Johannes Brahms, Versuch einer kritischen Dokumentar-Biographie*, 2 vols. (Bonn, 1997), p. 603.
[3] Max Kalbeck, *Johannes Brahms*, vol. II (Berlin, 1904-14), p. 366.
[4] Cite from Kross, *Johannes Brahms*, p. 604.
[5] Hermann Kretzschmar, *Neue Werke von J. Brahms*, part III, in: *Musikalisches Wochenblatt* 1874, No. 7, pp. 83-97.